T0393564

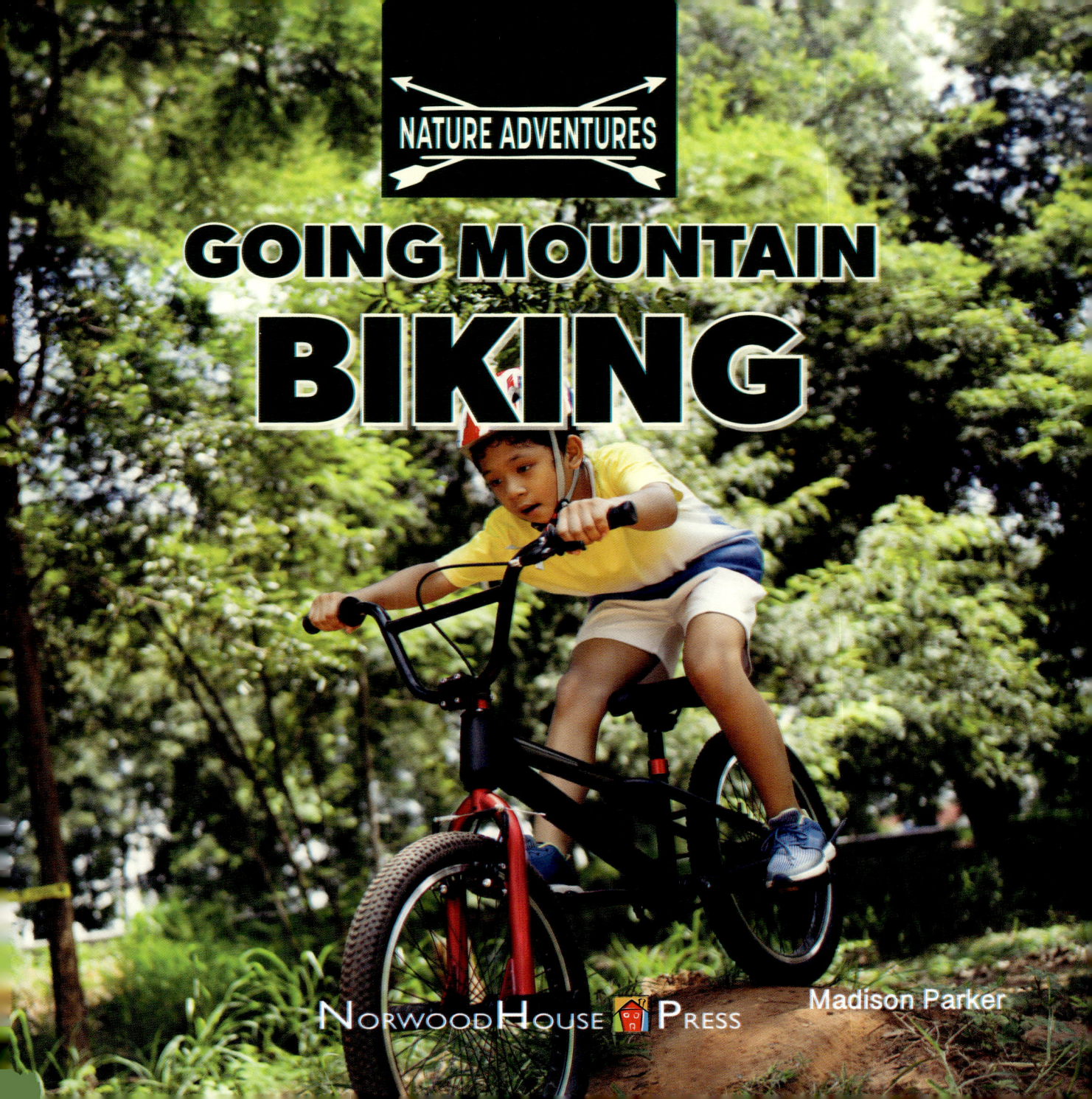

NATURE ADVENTURES

GOING MOUNTAIN BIKING

Norwood House Press

Madison Parker

Cataloging-in-Publication Data

Names: Parker, Madison.
Title: Going mountain biking / Madison Parker.
Description: Buffalo, NY : Norwood House Press, 2026. | Series: Nature adventures | Includes glossary and index.
Identifiers: ISBN 9781978574687 (pbk.) | ISBN 9781978574694 (library bound) | ISBN 9781978574700 (ebook)
Subjects: LCSH: Mountain biking--Juvenile literature.
Classification: LCC GV1056.P375 2026 | DDC 796.63--dc23

Published in 2026 by
Norwood House Press
2544 Clinton Street
Buffalo, NY 14224

Copyright © 2026 Norwood House Press
Designer: Rhea Magaro
Editor: Kim Thompson

Photo credits: Cover, p. 1, 6 Alexandra Golubtsova/Shutterstock.com; p. 5 Photobac/Shutterstock.com; p. 7 everst/Shutterstock.com; p. 9 JJ pixs/Shutterstock.com; p. 10 Alex Brylov/Shutterstock.com; pp. 11, 13 Soloviova Liudmyla/Shutterstock.com; pp. 12, 16 Sergey Novikov/Shutterstock.com; pp. 14, 15 zhukovvvlad/Shutterstock.com; p. 17 honzik7/Shutterstock.com; p. 18 Anna Nahabed/Shutterstock.com; p. 19 PiXel Perfect PiX/Shutterstock.com; p. 21 Melinda J Johnson/Shutterstock.com;

All rights reserved. No part of this book may be reproduced in any form without permission in writing from the publisher, except by a reviewer.

Printed in the United States of America

Some of the images in this book illustrate individuals who are models. The depictions do not imply actual situations or events.

CPSIA compliance information: Batch #CSNHP26: For further information contact Norwood House Press at 1-800-237-9932.

Find us on

TABLE OF CONTENTS

WHAT IS MOUNTAIN BIKING?

Let's go mountain biking! Mountain biking is a fun outdoor activity.

A mountain bike can ride over rough and rocky **terrain**. Many people like to have mountain biking adventures.

You can ride through forests and fields. You are surrounded by nature. There are many things to see!

MOUNTAIN BIKING SUPPLIES

You will need a mountain bike. Mountain bikes are different than regular bikes. They are taller. They have wider wheels. They have a sturdier **frame**.

Gloves protect your hands. They help you grip the **handlebars**. Sturdy shoes help you stay on the pedals.

A **helmet** is also very important. It protects your head in case you fall.

Mountain biking is challenging! It makes you tired and thirsty. It is important to bring water to drink.

Mountain biking is also **unpredictable**. Trails can be steep and rough. They can be muddy. Pack a first aid kit to use in case anyone gets hurt.

MOUNTAIN BIKING SAFETY

It is important to be careful when you go mountain biking. You must be aware of your **surroundings**. Be prepared to act quickly.

Mountain bikers should Leave No **Trace** (LNT). That means you should not leave trash or anything else behind.

Leave the **wilderness** better than you found it. This protects **wildlife**.

WHERE TO GO MOUNTAIN BIKING

You do not have to go mountain biking in the mountains. There are trails all around. You can even find indoor trails!

It is important to read any **regulations** before you go.

You can visit your state's park website to find trails near you. Mountain biking helps you explore the great outdoors!

Glossary

frame (frame): the strong metal part of a bike that holds it together

handlebars (HAN-duhl-bahrz): the parts you hold to control and steer a bike

helmet (HEL-mit): a hard hat that covers and protects your head

regulations (reg-yuh-LAY-shuhnz): rules you need to follow

surroundings (suh-ROUN-dingz): everything around you; the environment

terrain (tuh-RAYN): an area of ground

trace (trays): a sign that someone has been in a place; evidence

unpredictable (uhn-pri-DIK-tuh-buhl): likely to change suddenly and hard to know ahead of time

wilderness (WIL-dur-nis): wild land where no people live

wildlife (WILDE-life): wild animals living in their natural environment

Thinking Questions

1. What is mountain biking?

2. Describe mountain biking trails.

3. What should you bring on a mountain biking adventure?

4. How can you stay safe when you go mountain biking?

5. Where can you find mountain biking trails?

Index

About the Author

Madison Parker spent her childhood in the city of Chicago, Illinois. A farm girl at heart, today she lives in Wisconsin with her husband and four children on a small farm with cows, goats, chickens, and two miniature horses named Harley and David. Her favorite dessert is vanilla frozen custard with rainbow sprinkles, even in the winter.